DEDICATED TO THE LORD

Five Parental Promises for the
Faithful Discipleship of Children

Truth:78

Dedicated to the Lord—Five Parental Promises for the Faithful Discipleship of Children

By David Michael

Copyright © 2020 Next Generation Resources, Inc. Illustrations Truth78.

All rights reserved. No part of this publication may be reproduced in any form without written permission from Truth78.

Published in the United States by Truth78.

ISBN: 978-1-952783-15-9

All Scripture quotations, unless otherwise noted, are from the ESV © Bible (The Holy Bible, English Standard Version®), copyright © 2001 by Crossway, a publishing ministry of Good News Publishers. Used by permission. ESV Text Edition: 2016. Used by permission. All rights reserved.

Truth78.org · info@Truth78.org · 877.400.1414 · @Truth78org

Dedicated to the memory of

Grant Christopher Johnson

given to Steve and Laura on April 26, 1991

taken from them according to God's steadfast love and glorious purposes on July 23, 1991

in the certain hope that he now belongs wholly to Jesus Christ, forever.

Blessed be the name of the Lord! (Job 1:21)

Table of Contents

Dedicated to the Lord—Five Parental Promises for the 7
  Faithful Discipleship of Children
    Child Dedication—A Working Definition 8

Promises of Dedication 13
    Promise 1: To acknowledge our children as gifts of God 13
    Promise 2: To surrender worldly claims on our children 14
    Promise 3: To bring up our children in the discipline 22
        and instruction of the Lord.
    Promise 4: To provide for our children 31
    Promise 5: To pray for the salvation of our children 41

A Time for Commitment and Dedication 47

Appendix
    "Exposition of Ephesians 6:4" by John Piper 53
    Recommended Resources 57
    Truth78 65

Five Parental Promises for the Faithful Discipleship of Children

In 1982, and again in 1985, Sally and I stood before our brothers and sisters in Christ, a new baby in our arms, and made five promises in a special service of dedication. Then in 2005, in what seemed like a blink of an eye, and again in 2008 and 2011, I was standing before my eldest daughter, her husband, and their brothers and sisters in Christ, with each of our grandchildren in their arms, making the same five promises in similar services of dedication.

Over the years, I have had the privilege of standing before hundreds of parents as the words of the same five promises have taken root in my own heart, the hearts of those parents, and the hearts of the people in the two congregations that I have served. These promises have been a consistent reminder to Sally and me of the high and holy calling upon our lives as parents, while serving as a foundation for our ministry to parents and children in those churches. Countless times, I have reminded parents of these promises for their encouragement in various seasons of their lives. The promises have also served as a regular reminder to both congregations of our corporate responsibility as God's people to support and participate in the efforts of the church to invest in the faith and the discipleship of the next generation.

This little book is an attempt to unpack the significance, meaning, and implication of each of the five promises. As helpful as I hope it will be to parents who are preparing to make these promises, the benefit is not limited to using them in a church's child dedication service. I am hoping this resource will also serve those parents who are not part of a church tradition that practices child dedication or a church that does not use these specific promises as part of its dedication services.

Though the five promises have been at the center of a precious tradition in the churches that I served, they represent the biblical calling and responsibility that rests on all Christian parents who have been entrusted with children to raise for the glory of their Creator. Whether we stand before our brothers and sisters in Christ and make these promises or not, we will all one day stand before our King of kings and Lord of lords. On that great day, may God find us to be faithful servants and stewards of the precious gifts that He has entrusted to us.

Child Dedication—A Working Definition

The dedication of children is an act of faith in the presence of God and His people in which we solemnly and earnestly offer our children up to God for His wise and sovereign purposes in their lives, and offer ourselves up to God for the holy responsibility of being biblical parents and raising our children in the fear, knowledge, and joy of the Lord.

I will unpack this definition more and refer to it as we look closely at the five promises. However, before going any further, I want to acknowledge at the outset that this definition and the wording for each of the promises were crafted by John Piper in his first year of pastoral ministry at Bethlehem Baptist Church. Except for a couple of modest adjustments, the promises are the same as they were when John presided over his first dedication service more than 40 years ago.

> **Whether we stand before our brothers and sisters in Christ and make these promises or not, we will all one day stand before our King of kings and Lord of lords. On that great day, may God find us to be faithful servants and stewards of the precious gifts that He has entrusted to us.**

To set the stage for the examination of the promises, I want first to address four common questions concerning the dedication of children.

1. What are the historical roots of child dedications?

Child dedication dates back to at least the 18th century.[1] Its origin is unclear, but it was likely established as an alternative practice for churches that rejected paedobaptism (infant baptism). It is most commonly practiced in churches that also practice believer's baptism.[2]

Theological and historical convictions aside, it is appropriate to respond to the birth of a child in a way that acknowledges the person-forming work of God. The christening or baptism of infants was not only the application of particular church doctrine, but it also provided the opportunity to celebrate the creation and blessing of new life and offered a time for parents to commit themselves to faithfully raise their children in the faith. Most likely, the rejection of infant baptism created a significant void in the church that the dedication of children filled.

T. L. Underwood noted that for "Christians who adopted an anti-paedobaptist position in the Reformation Era, two practical questions presented themselves. First, ought they themselves to be re-baptized as believers, or was their first baptism as infants sufficient? Secondly, ought some type of dedicatory service ... be performed for their children who would not be baptized until [later] ... ?"[3]

It was in answer to that second question that the dedication service was established and is still commonly practiced today in churches that practice only adult or believer's baptism.

---

1 Worship Training. "Historical Origins and Development of Child Dedication," copyright © 2020 Worship Training, worshiptraining.com. www.worshiptraining.com) at: https://www.worshiptraining.com/media/historical-origins-and-development-of-child-dedication

2 Those who practice believer's baptism teach that a person should be baptized when that person is able to give a credible profession of faith in Jesus Christ.

3 T. L. Underwood, "Child Dedication Services in the 17th Century," *Baptist Quarterly 23.4* (October 1969): 165. (Past Editions of the Baptist Quarterly can be accessed at https://biblicalstudies.org.uk/articles_bq_08.php#vol23)

2. Does the Bible teach that parents must dedicate their children?

Three of the most common passages in the Bible that have been used to support the practice of child dedication in the church are 1 Samuel 1:27-28 (Hannah presenting Samuel at the temple after he was weaned), Luke 2:22-24 (Joseph and Mary presenting Jesus at the temple), and Mark 10:16 (Jesus blessing the children):

And he took them in his arms and blessed them, laying his hands on them.

It would be difficult to make a strong case from these or other biblical texts for requiring the dedication of children in the church, just as it would be difficult to make a case for forbidding it. However, there are good, biblical reasons why I have encouraged parents to dedicate their children and have recommended occasional dedication services in the church. The following are some of those reasons:

- It is fitting in the context of corporate worship to glorify God and praise Him for His amazing, person-forming work and His gracious generosity and creative power (Psalm 111:1-2; Psalm 145:10-12).
- It is an opportunity for parents and the church to publicly acknowledge our children as gifts of God, to celebrate His blessing, and to give thanks to Him for these gifts (Job 1:21; Romans 11:34-36; Psalm 127:3).
- It is an act of surrender and submission to God and His will for our children, who were ultimately created for His glory and His purposes (Isaiah 43:6-7; Isaiah 46:9-11; Ephesians 1:3-4).
- It is a declaration of parental and congregational commitment to be examples of godliness and to raise our children in the fear, knowledge, and joy of the Lord (Deuteronomy 6:6-7, 20-21; Ephesians 6:4).
- It is a corporate appeal to God for His grace for the sake of our children in the hope that they will be in Christ,

holy and blameless before the Lord (Ephesians 1:4) and belong wholly to Him forever (1 Thessalonians 4:17).

3. What practical benefit does a public dedication have for parents and the church?

- Calling people to make public their resolve to faithfulness and obedience as parents encourages them to be faithful and obedient.
- It reinforces in the church a biblical understanding of children and our corporate responsibility to pray for, encourage, and model Christlikeness for them.
- It provides a focal point and a significant event for parents to remember and to build upon as they welcome a child into their home.
- It serves as a reminder for all of the parents in the congregation of the solemn responsibility that they have as parents and provides an opportunity for them to strengthen their resolve to parental faithfulness.

4. Should parents dedicate only their babies?

Regardless of a child's age, parents should feel the freedom to "offer [their] children up to God for His wise and sovereign purposes in their lives and offer [themselves] up to God for the holy responsibility of being biblical parents and raising [their] children in the fear, knowledge, and joy of the Lord."[4]

Parents who are part of a church that practices child dedication will usually dedicate their children within the first three years of life. However, it is not uncommon for parents to dedicate children as old as eight or nine, especially when they did not have the opportunity to do so when their children were younger.

Let's turn our attention now to the five dedication promises and consider their significance and relevance for any Christian parent, whether or not they officially make these promises or publicly dedicate their children in the church.

---

4 See "Child Dedication—A Working Definition" on page 8.

Promises of Dedication

Promise 1: To acknowledge our children as gifts of God.

Do you recognize this child as a gift of God and give heartfelt thanks for God's blessing?

"Behold, children are a gift of the LORD . . ." (Psalm 127:3 NASB) for "from him and through him and to him are all things" (Romans 11:36). In this first promise, we recognize and honor God as the One who has given us our children.

At first glance, it would seem there is no need to make this promise. Of course, our children are gifts of God. Only the most atheistic parents could witness the birth of a child and exalt themselves or an attending physician as the creators and sustainers of a life that did not exist 10 months prior. As adoptive parents, Sally and I were not present for the birth of our two daughters, but we were still in awe as we received these two precious souls who were known by God before the foundation of the world (Ephesians 1:4), knit together in their mothers' wombs (Psalm 139:13), and led into our home and hearts by the mountain-moving hand of God (Isaiah 46:9-11). When the time came to dedicate our daughters, we had no trouble whole-heartedly affirming this promise.

Still, parental resolve to keep this promise can be tested more than we might think. There are times and seasons when it is difficult to recognize or accept a child as a gift. When making this promise, parents resolve by God's grace to always recognize and affirm their children as gifts and always give thanks to God for them.

Children are a gift regardless of the timing and circumstances of their arrival. They are a gift when they arrive before the completion of graduate school, before the loans are paid off, and after losing a job. They are a gift—not a problem, not an accident, not an inconvenience, and not a disruption to plans.

> **Children are a gift even when they are not what we expected or hoped for.**

Children are a gift even when they are not what we expected or hoped for. They are a gift when they come with infantile seizures, chromosome irregularities, heart problems, deformities, blindness, tumors, brain damage, respiratory issues, and any number of physical, psychological, or emotional realities that require extraordinary parental care, attention, and resources.

Every child comes to us as a sinner. When we see evidence of their depravity, we must remind ourselves and each other of this promise. They are gifts when they refuse to go to sleep, spill their milk, throw their food on the floor, display their temper in the grocery store, ignore parental instruction, rebel against authority, run away from home, get arrested for shoplifting, or even worse.

Though it is not always easy, this first promise is a commitment to recognize children as blessings from God and give heartfelt thanks for the privilege of being entrusted by their Creator with the responsibility to raise them in the fear, discipline, and joy of the Lord.

Promise 2: To surrender worldly claims on our children.

Do you dedicate this child to the Lord who gave him/her to you, surrendering all worldly claims upon his/her life in the hope that he/she will belong wholly to Jesus Christ?

Of the five promises, none carries more significance for me as a parent and pastor than this one. Sally and I have had to remind each other of it often. I have also had many opportunities to remind parents of this significant promise in my years of ministry. You will understand why as we carefully consider the three key phrases in this promise:

1. "Do you dedicate this child to the Lord . . . ?"

Let's go back to our definition and look closely at the meaning of dedication. First, note that the dedication of a child is "an act of faith" on the part of the parents.[5] In faith, we entrust our children to the grace of God, who sustains every breath and every heartbeat in our children (Hebrews 1:3, Psalm 3:5). Only God, through Christ, can ultimately deliver them from the "domain of darkness" in which they are born and transfer them to the "kingdom of his beloved" (Colossians 1:13). As we will see in Promise 3, parents play a key role in God's unfolding purposes for their children. When making this promise, parents acknowledge that, apart from God, they can do nothing.

As we dedicate our children, it is important to keep in mind that we are trusting God not only for the faith of our children, but also for the faith of our grandchildren and every subsequent generation so that they too should "set their hope in God" (Psalm 78:7).

The definition further emphasizes that dedication should be done solemnly and earnestly. It is not a mere tradition or formality for honoring the birth of a child, but rather a serious commitment to God. Though dedication promises do not quite rise to the same level as marriage vows, the words of institution for a traditional wedding ceremony provide a fitting admonition for those dedicating their children—that these promises should not be made "unadvisedly or lightly, but reverently, deliberately, soberly, in the fear of God . . . "[6]

Making these dedication promises in the presence of God and His people affirms our accountability to God and His people. It acknowledges the presence of those who are there to support, encourage, and pray for the parents. The people in the congregation are also reminded of their God-given responsibility for the faithful discipleship of the next generation.

---

5 See "Child Dedication—A Working Definition" on page 8.

6 Quoted from the Words of Institution adapted from the Anglican *Book of Common Prayer: Solemnization of Matrimony*, 1662.

2. " . . . surrendering all worldly claims upon his/her life . . . "

> **As citizens of heaven, however, we are preparing our children for God's Kingdom, not our own.**

For generations, parents have been able to successfully claim the right to control the care and upbringing of their children. As citizens of this world, we ought to preserve, protect, and resist any effort to usurp this sacred parental right. As citizens of heaven, however, we are preparing our children for God's Kingdom, not our own. By faith, we surrender our ambitions for our children, our personal comfort, and all other "worldly claim" to God "for His wise and sovereign purposes in their lives."[7]

While our children are gifts from God to us, they, along with everything else in the universe, belong to God (Psalm 50:10-12). He has entrusted our children to us while retaining sovereign rights over them. In other words, God gives us our children, but He keeps the ultimate claim on their lives.

As we make this promise, it is important that we consider three of the specific rights God retains:

1) **The right to give our children and take them from us according to His "wise and sovereign purposes" for them and for us.**

Before our children took their first breaths, God established when their last ones would be.

> *Your eyes saw my unformed substance; in your book were written, every one of them, the days that were formed for me, when as yet there were none of them (Psalm 139:16).*

On the day when Job was informed that all of his children had perished (along with practically everything else he

---

[7] See "Child Dedication—A Working Definition" on page 8.

possessed) he "arose and tore his robe and shaved his head and fell on the ground and worshiped" (Job 1:20).

> *And [Job] said, "Naked I came from my mother's womb, and naked I shall return. The LORD gave, and the LORD has taken away; blessed be the name of the LORD" (Job 1:21).*

When the Lord gives, it is easy to worship our good and gracious Giver. When that same infinitely wise, steadfastly loving, eternally good Giver is pleased to take a child sooner than we expect, we humbly lay our hands over our mouths and worship.[8]

On Sunday, July 7, 1991, Steve and Laura Johnson stood before the congregation of Bethlehem Baptist Church of Minneapolis, Minnesota holding their second-born, 10-week-old Grant Christopher. Along with six other couples, Steve and Laura "solemnly and earnestly" made these five promises before God and their brothers and sisters in Christ. Eighteen days later they were standing in the same room, in the same spot; only this time they were not holding Grant in their arms. Instead, his lifeless body lay in a little white casket. Two days before, Grant had gone down for his nap and stopped breathing. As we met and prayed in the hospital emergency room, the phrase that Steve and Laura kept repeating through tears was, "we surrender worldly claim upon his life."

Certainly, Steve and Laura did not expect their son's life to be so short, but in the moment of heart-breaking loss, they kept their promise, entrusting their son by faith to the wisdom of a good and gracious God who had given him to them. One of the reasons making this promise can be so hard is because we don't know how we would respond

---

8 This is an allusion to the words of Sarah Edwards, who after her husband Jonathan's sudden and unexpected death wrote these words to her daughter, Esther: "My Very Dear Child, What shall I say? A holy and good God has covered us with a dark cloud. O that we may kiss the rod, and lay our hands on our mouths! The Lord has done it. He has made me adore his goodness, that we had him so long. But my God lives; and he has my heart" (Edna Gerstner, *Jonathan and Sarah: An Uncommon Union* [Morgan, Penn.: Soli Deo Gloria, 1995], 223.)

if faced with such sorrow. Three weeks before the funeral, Steve and Laura would not have known either. They made the promise by faith, trusting that God's grace would be there, and it was.

2) The right to lead our children wherever He pleases.

The book of 1 Samuel opens with the familiar account of Hannah, married to Elkanah, and childless. Year after year after year, Hannah traveled to Shiloh with her husband for the annual sacrifice. Each year, she pleaded with the Lord to open her womb, and each year it remained closed until the moment had come for God to act. Once again, as they had done so many times before, the couple arrived in Shiloh. This time Hannah, "was deeply distressed and prayed to the Lord and wept bitterly. And she vowed a vow and said 'O LORD of hosts, if you will indeed look on the affliction of your servant and remember me and not forget your servant, but will give to your servant a son, then I will give him to the LORD all the days of his life" (1 Samuel 1:10-11).

God heard her prayer, and "in due time Hannah conceived and bore a son, and she called his name Samuel, for she said, 'I have asked for him from the LORD'... And when she had weaned him, she took [Samuel] up with her... and she brought him to the house of the LORD at Shiloh... and they brought the child to Eli. And she said, '... For this child I prayed, and the LORD has granted me my petition... Therefore I have lent him to the LORD. As long as he lives, he is lent to the LORD.' And [Samuel] worshiped the LORD there" while Hannah returned home, without her child (1 Samuel 1:20, 24, 25-28).

As much as Hannah longed for a child, and as much joy and comfort Samuel undoubtedly brought to her in the short time he was with her, she surrendered her God-given desires to God's greater purpose for Samuel and for Israel. In the same way, we surrender our desires and joyfully entrust our children to the One who created them "for His wise and sovereign purposes in their lives."[9]

On June 28, 1819, in Bradford, Massachusetts, Adoniram Judson presented himself for missionary service in the East to the American Board of Commissioners for Foreign Missions. On that same day, he met and fell in love with Ann Hasseltine, a member of the church that hosted the event. After knowing Ann for one month, Adoniram boldly expressed his intentions in a letter to John Hasseltine, Ann's father. For the fathers of daughters reading this, imagine receiving this letter from a young man who just met your daughter a month ago:

> *I have now to ask, whether you can consent to part with your daughter early next spring, to see her no more in this world; whether you can consent to her departure, and her subjection to the hardships and sufferings of missionary life; whether you can consent to her exposure to the dangers of the ocean, to the fatal influence of the southern climate of India; to every kind of want and distress; to degradation, insult, persecution, and perhaps a violent death.*
>
> *Can you consent to all this, for the sake of him who left his heavenly home, and died for her and for you; for the sake of perishing, immortal souls; for the sake of Zion, and the glory of God? Can you consent to all this, in hope of soon meeting your daughter in the world of glory, with the crown of righteousness, brightened with the acclamations of praise which shall redound to her Savior from heathens saved, through her means, from eternal woe and despair?*[10]

---

9 See "Child Dedication—A Working Definition" on page 8.

10 John Piper, "How Few There Are Who Die So Hard! Suffering and Success in the Life of Adoniram Judson: The Cost of Bringing Christ to Burma." 2003 Bethlehem Conference for Pastors. Minneapolis, Minnesota. February 4, 2003. Available online at: https://www.desiringgod.org/messages/how-few-there-are-who-die-so-hard

John told Adoniram that Ann could make up her own mind. Her response is captured in a letter to her friend Lydia Kimball:

> *I feel willing, and expect, if nothing in Providence prevents, to spend my days in this world in heathen lands. Yes, Lydia, I have about come to the determination to give up all my comforts and enjoyments here, sacrifice my affection to relatives and friends, and go where God, in his Providence, shall see fit to place me.*[11]

As hard as it would be for a parent to embrace the implications of such a decision, there can also be great joy seeing their child walking in truth and in joyful submission to the purposes of our wise and sovereign King.

Ann married Judson on February 5, 1812. Two weeks later, at age 23, she left with him on the boat for India. All three of Adoniram and Ann's children died. The first was stillborn as the couple sailed from India to Burma. The second, Roger William Judson, lived for 17 months and died. Their third, Maria Elizabeth Butterworth Judson, made it to her second birthday and outlived her mother by six months. Ann died of smallpox in Lower Burma at age 37.[12]

God's Kingdom purposes for Ann mattered more than whatever personal desires her parents may have had for her—they *surrendered* Ann to those purposes and *all worldly claim upon her life*. The Lord may see fit to keep our children and grandchildren close to us, or He may be pleased to invest their lives in a place on the other side of the country or on the other side of the world. He may lead them to a dangerous neighborhood or a beachside resort community. Our children may follow the Lord to a place where they may be tempted by extraordinary comfort or a place where they will be subjected to the "hardships and sufferings of missionary life" and exposure to dangers and "fatal influence." As parents, we may have to endure our children suffering distress,

---

11 Ibid.
12 Ibid.

"degradation, insult, persecution, and perhaps a violent death." Whatever our wise and sovereign God may have for them, . . . we surrender worldly claim upon their lives.

3) **The right to bring our children to faith according to His purposes, in His way, and on His timetable.**

Christian parents desire for their children to trust and treasure Christ when they are young and faithfully follow Him all of their lives. However, Christian parents also know that this is not always the way children come to faith in Christ. Some children will step onto a path of foolishness, rebellion, and unbelief. They may face serious consequences from bad decisions that God, in His wisdom, will use to deliver them from their rebellious hearts. It may take an abusive relationship, a failed marriage, addictions, crime, a crisis pregnancy, or another difficult circumstance before their eyes are opened to the beauty of Christ. God may use the very things we fear the most to bring our children to saving faith. If He does, we, by faith, surrender worldly claim on their lives to God who is free to accomplish His wise and sovereign purposes for our children. We submit to whenever, wherever, and whatever those purposes require, which leads us to the final phrase of this promise.

3. " . . . in the hope that he/she will belong wholly to Jesus Christ."

Ultimately, nothing is more important to our children than belonging wholly to Jesus Christ. Salvation is only possible through the transforming power of God by His grace through Jesus Christ (Luke 18:27). The heart of the king and the hearts of our children are like a stream of water in the hand of the Lord (Proverbs 21:1). Nothing is outside the power of God to turn a heart wherever He will. Nothing can thwart God's purposes, not even the heart of the most rebellious child.

I was given a beautiful picture of this ultimate hope several years ago in the waiting room of a local hospital. I arrived at 6 a.m. and was greeted by parents whose infant son was scheduled for surgery to correct a congenital heart defect. In the gaps between the various pre-op procedures and conversations with members of the surgical team, the parents and I talked, shared Scripture, and prayed. At about 6:45 a.m., the anesthesiologist entered and announced that they were ready. With tears, the mother laid her precious son into the arms of the physician. As he turned, he said, "We'll take good care of him" and disappeared through the door. Since that experience, I have had an image of what it means to surrender our children to God *in hope*. Because that little boy needed what his parents could not provide, they entrusted him to One who could.

Because our children need what we ultimately cannot provide, we dedicate them, we surrender worldly claim, and we entrust them to the only One who can, in hope that they will belong wholly to Jesus Christ, forever.

Promise 3: To bring up our children in the discipline and instruction of the Lord.

Do you pledge, with God's fatherly help, to bring up your child in the discipline and instruction of the Lord, making every reasonable effort, with faithfulness, patience, and love, to build the Word of God, the character of Christ, and the joy of the Lord into his/her life?

Discipline and Instruction

We "offer ourselves up to God for the holy responsibility of being biblical parents and raising our children in the fear, knowledge, and joy of the Lord"[13] The biblical foundation for this promise is Paul's instruction in Ephesians 6:4, "Fathers, do not provoke your children to anger, but bring them up in the discipline and instruction of the Lord."[14]

The Bible teaches that children, like all human beings, have inherited a sin nature. David acknowledges this in Psalm 51:5, "Behold, I was brought forth in iniquity, and in sin did my mother

---

13 See "Child Dedication—A Working Definition" on page 8.

14 For a fuller exposition of this verse and its application to this promise, see the Appendix for a portion of John Piper's helpful article, "Exposition on Ephesians 6:4."

conceive me." Parents do not have to teach their children to be selfish, to lie, or to have temper tantrums. The inherited sin nature, at work in every child's heart, is the root of all sinful behavior (Romans 5:12; Luke 6:45). Therefore, our discipline needs to address the real problem—their sinful hearts that incline them to do wrong things (Genesis 6:5; Jeremiah 17:9)—rather than simply address their wrong behavior. They are sinners in need of grace. They have sinful hearts (Genesis 6:5; Jeremiah 17:9), which are naturally inclined toward sin instead of righteousness. But children are entrusted to parents who are called to train their sinful hearts in righteousness. Even though discipline is often perceived as negative, it is better understood positively in the larger context of discipleship and training in righteousness (Hebrews 12:7-11).

> **As sinners ourselves, parents must rely on God's grace to give us the patience and love to discipline our children with a wisdom and firmness that are tempered with love.**

Faithful parental discipline also lays the groundwork for a healthy fear of the Lord, yielding fruitfulness and blessing in a person's life. Children must acknowledge that God is the Creator and sovereign Ruler of the universe. Unlike God, they are created beings who are to live in awe and respect of Him, submitting to His desires and commands.

When we correct misbehavior and sinful attitudes in our children, we are demonstrating to them that disobedience is wrong and that respect for authority is right. We are also helping to train their hearts through consequences and to bend their wills toward submission to God's authority. Most importantly, we are laying essential foundations for the gospel as children grow in their understanding of sin and the depravity of the human heart, the need for repentance, forgiveness, and reconciliation, and their desperate need for justification and righteousness through Christ Jesus. As sinners ourselves, parents must rely on God's grace to give us the patience and love to discipline our children with a wisdom and firmness that are tempered with love.

Our children have inherited a conscience and have a general knowledge of God as revealed through creation (Romans 1:19-20), but only when they embrace the gospel and trust Christ can they be truly transformed. They must be taught the truth and come to understand the gospel as revealed in the written Word of God. This third promise affirms the privilege and responsibility we have been given for the instruction of our children.

Fathers as Shepherds

As both parents embrace their responsibility for the discipline and instruction of their children, it is important to note that in Ephesians 6:4, Paul emphasizes that fathers are especially accountable. For Paul, the father's shepherding role in the home parallels an elder's shepherding in the church.

We can see this parallel in 1 Timothy 3:4-5 where Paul includes in his list of qualifications for an elder that he "manage his household well ... for if someone does not know how to manage his own household, how will he care for God's church?" The word "manage" literally means, "to stand before," as in "to lead, protect, and provide." Paul suggests that this shepherding care is what both fathers and elders are called to, and therefore if a man does not faithfully shepherd his own household, we should not assume he would be able to shepherd the church.

Seeing the parallel relationship between shepherding at home and shepherding at church can help us better understand our responsibility as fathers. Even though Timothy Witmer's insightful book, *The Shepherd Leader: Achieving Effective Shepherding in Your Church,* was written for church shepherds, it provides valuable insights for the father-shepherd. According to Witmer, four simple words encompass the biblical responsibility of a shepherd—Know, Feed, Lead, and Protect. Father-shepherds would be well-served by taking the time to understand each of these responsibilities and to consider how to fulfill them in the household.

It would be difficult to overemphasize the indispensability of a mother's role in the discipleship of the children and how utterly crucial it is for both parents to be of one mind and heart as they fulfill the God-given calling on their lives. Much of what I would want to say about the significant role that mothers have in the discipleship of their children has already been written by my wife in *Mothers: Disciplers of the Next Generations*.[15] I heartily commend this rich source of biblical wisdom and practical helpfulness to both mothers and their husbands.

It is my earnest prayer that every father who makes this third promise will, in partnership with his wife, initiate and lead the efforts in his home to intentionally instruct each child in the truth; instill a biblical, God-centered orientation to all of life; commend the example of Christ; and show his children the path that leads to everlasting life—all in a manner characterized by Christ-like faithfulness, patience, and love.

" . . . with God's fatherly help . . . "

These four hope-giving words are a precious part of this promise. I don't know that I could have kept this promise without them. On the evening before He was crucified, Jesus assured His disciples that "apart from me you can do nothing" (John 15:5). The mindset that Jesus wanted His disciples to have is the mindset we must have as parents. Apart from God's fatherly help, we cannot bring our children up "in the discipline and instruction of the Lord" any more than we can "build the Word of God, the character of Christ, and the joy of the Lord" into their lives.

While assuring the disciples of their helplessness, Jesus was emphasizing the importance and the hope of abiding in Him, saying:

> *"Abide in me, and I in you. As the branch cannot bear fruit by itself, unless it abides in the vine, neither can you unless you abide in me" (John 15:4).*

---

15 Sally Michael, *Mothers: Disciplers of the Next Generations* (Minneapolis, Minn.: Truth78, 2013).

In case we missed the point, He makes clear in the next verse, "Whoever abides in me and I in him, he it is that bears much fruit." We make this third promise with a heart to be faithful and fruitful parents, neither of which we will be without "God's fatherly help" through Jesus Christ.

In that same discourse, just 10 verses earlier, Jesus assured His disciples that He would be leaving them, but He would not leave them without a Helper to "teach [them] all things" and "to be with [them] forever" (John 14:26). That same Helper stands with us as we pledge our faithfulness as parents, and abides with us forever to teach us and to equip us with everything we need to be fruitful.

"…making every reasonable effort…"

As true as it is that we can do nothing apart from "God's fatherly help," we must still put forth "every reasonable effort." The Bible makes an important connection between God's grace and our works. We see this connection clearly when Paul instructs the Philippians to "work out your own salvation with fear and trembling, **for** it is God who works in you, both to will and to work for his good pleasure" (Philippians 2:12-13). As with our own salvation, so also we should work for the salvation of our children. To say it another way, we should disciple them. We can do this with hope and confidence "**for**" indeed, God is at work "both to will and to work for his good pleasure" in them.

When considering this third promise, it is important to understand that we can promise to be faithful parents, and we can rely on God's fatherly help, but we cannot guarantee the results of our efforts. Not every child who grows up with the loving, patient instruction and discipline of Christian parents becomes a true disciple. As parents, we can faithfully instruct our children in the truth, but we cannot make them embrace the truth.

For decades, Sally and I have encouraged and equipped parents for intentionality, seriousness, thoughtfulness, earnestness, and faithfulness concerning the discipleship of their children. As we offered vision, guiding principles, and practical strategies, we cautioned parents not to presume that if they faithfully follow their plan, their children will necessarily become followers of Christ. This is a defective and dangerous conclusion for two reasons. First, it neglects and offends the sovereignty of God over the souls of our children. Secondly, it sets parents up for sinful pride or unnecessary guilt and shame. If a child flourishes in faith and walks in the truth, the parents may be tempted to take more credit than they should. More often, when a child forsakes Christ and fails to walk in the truth, parents are often quick to assume they must have failed or done something wrong. All parents can look back on mistakes they have made in raising their children, but those mistakes cannot hinder God from accomplishing His saving purposes in their children's lives.

This emphasis on the sovereignty of God over the salvation of our children and our God-given responsibility as parents for the discipleship of our children raises an important question: What motivation or hope is there in faithfully instructing and discipling our children if, in the end, they remain in their unbelief? Or, to ask it another way: If the spiritual neglect of our children won't keep God from accomplishing His saving work in our children, why should we do all of this work? I'd like to offer some help for dealing with this tension:

1) **It is God who saves.** Our first response to these questions must be to simply affirm what we know to be true. Since God's Word is clear on our responsibility, we must be faithful to what God calls us to do, while relying on His grace to do it, and trusting Him to accomplish what we can't.

2) **Obedience has a profound impact.** Parental obedience and faithfulness often is the means of spiritual blessing for children. Noah, for example, was "a righteous man." He "walked with God," was righteous before God, and was "blameless in his generation" (Genesis 6:9; Genesis 7:1). The Bible does not tell us anything about the faith of Shem, Ham, Japheth, or the rest of the family, but it does make clear that it was because of Noah's righteousness that his household was spared judgment: "By faith Noah, being warned by God concerning events as yet unseen, in reverent fear constructed an ark for the saving of his household" (Hebrews 11:7).

Abraham also was "counted" righteous (Genesis 15:6; Romans 4:3,13), and through his righteousness his offspring were blessed (Genesis 17:7,8,19; Romans 4:13). In Genesis 18:19, God states His intention to accomplish His purpose and fulfill His promise to Abraham through the instruction of his "children and household": "For I have chosen him that he may command his children and his household after him to keep the way of the LORD by doing righteousness and justice, so that the LORD may bring to Abraham what he has promised him" (Genesis 18:19).

In the record of the kings of Judah and Israel, we find a number of examples where parental obedience influenced the next generation. "Solomon loved the LORD, walking in the statutes of David his father" (1 Kings 3:3). Jehoshaphat, son of Asa, "walked in all the way of Asa his father . . . doing what was right in the sight of the LORD" (1 Kings 22:43). Jotham, the son of Uzziah, "did what was right in the eyes of the LORD, according to all that his father Uzziah had done" (2 Kings 15:34).

Paul highlights two generations of parental influence in Timothy's life when he tells his young son in the faith, "I am reminded of your sincere faith, a faith that dwelt first in your grandmother Lois and your mother Eunice and now, I am sure, dwells in you as well" (2 Timothy 1:5).

In addition to the biblical examples, we ought to be encouraged by the testimony of many Christians whom God brought to faith through the influence of parents who raised them to know, fear, trust, and delight in the Lord.

3) **Disobedience has a profound impact.** We can also find a number of biblical examples where you can see the influence of parental wickedness and disobedience on subsequent generations. We can see this most clearly in the record of the kings of Israel and Judah. "Amon . . . did what was evil in the sight of the LORD, as Manasseh his father had done. He walked in all the way in which his father walked and served the idols that his father served and worshiped them. He abandoned the LORD, the God of his fathers, and did not walk in the way of the LORD" (2 Kings 21:19-22). The notorious Ahab was the son of Omri, who "did what was evil

in the sight of the LORD" (1 Kings 16:25). Ahab likewise "did evil in the sight of the LORD, more than all who were before him" (1 Kings 16:30). So also, Ahab's son-in-law, Ahaziah, "walked in the way of the house of Ahab and did what was evil in the sight of the LORD" (2 Kings 8:27).

4) **Parental faith is not deterministic.** Clearly, we see how parental faith, or lack thereof, influences children for better or worse, but it does not determine the faith of the child. God works His saving purposes both through and in spite of parental influence. Ahaziah's son, Jehoash, was seven years old when he took the throne after his father's death. It is interesting to note that he "did what was right in the eyes of the LORD all his days, because Jehoiada the priest instructed him" (2 Kings 12:2). Similarly, the priest Eli's two sons were "worthless men" who did not "know the LORD" (1 Samuel 2:12), and whose legendary abominations brought judgment on Eli's house for subsequent generations.

> **As parents, we are not held accountable for our children's response to faithful instruction and discipline. But we are accountable for our faithfulness to God and the responsibility He has given us to teach, train, correct, and pray for our children.**

Our obedience and faithfulness to God is not what saves our children. Neither does our disobedience nor our unfaithfulness necessarily bring judgment upon them. It is God who saves, God who blesses, God who judges, and God who condemns. However, our obedience to God and our faithfulness as parents is very often the means by which God saves our children. Conversely, it is our disobedience to God and unfaithfulness as parents that often keeps our children under God's wrath and leads to their condemnation. Blessed are those faithful parents whose children walk in the faith of their fathers

(3 John 1:4), and woe to unfaithful parents whose neglect tempts their children to stumble in unbelief (Luke 17:1-2).

As parents, we are not held accountable for our children's response to faithful instruction and discipline. But we are accountable for our faithfulness to God and the responsibility He has given us to teach, train, correct, and pray for our children. This parental responsibility and accountability can be compared to the watchman in Israel as described in Ezekiel 3:17-21.[16] The watchman's duty was to stand on the wall of the city and be alert to "the sword coming"—namely anything that would put the people in danger. If he "sees the sword coming" (see Ezekiel 33) and warns the people, he is faithful to his calling, even if the people fail to heed his warning and die. However, if the sword comes and the watchman fails to warn the people because of his unfaithfulness and neglect, he is held accountable for their deaths.

Promise 3 is a commitment to be a faithful watchman over the souls of our children. Our job is to make every effort to instruct and discipline our children in an atmosphere of faithfulness, patience, and love. Then we trust in the "fatherly help" and faithfulness of the One who gave us our children, rules over their hearts, and is able to lead them to saving faith and everlasting life. We take heart in the assurance that our success as Christian parents matters more to God than it does to us. God's reputation as the One who preserves faith in each generation is at stake, and we have all the resources of heaven to help us to faithfully and successfully fulfill God's calling on our lives.

---

[16] *Ezekiel 3:17-21*—"Son of man, I have made you a watchman for the house of Israel. Whenever you hear a word from my mouth, you shall give them warning from me. [18]*If I say to the wicked, 'You shall surely die,' and you give him no warning, nor speak to warn the wicked from his wicked way, in order to save his life, that wicked person shall die for his iniquity, but his blood I will require at your hand. [19]But if you warn the wicked, and he does not turn from his wickedness, or from his wicked way, he shall die for his iniquity, but you will have delivered your soul. [20]Again, if a righteous person turns from his righteousness and commits injustice, and I lay a stumbling block before him, he shall die. Because you have not warned him, he shall die for his sin, and his righteous deeds that he has done shall not be remembered, but his blood I will require at your hand. [21]But if you warn the righteous person not to sin, and he does not sin, he shall surely live, because he took warning, and you will have delivered your soul."

Promise 4: To provide for our children.

Do you promise to provide, through God's blessing, for the physical, emotional, intellectual, and spiritual needs of your child, looking to your own heavenly Father for the wisdom, love, and strength to serve and not use him/her?

This promise affirms parental responsibility to care for our children completely and in every way—physically, emotionally, intellectually, and spiritually. Like Promise 3, this promise would also be impossible to keep without these two qualifying statements: "through God's blessing" and "looking to your own heavenly Father for the wisdom."

God's blessings include medical services, schools, parks, recreation, activities, and services of various kinds that can help us keep our children healthy in all of these areas. Many books, some of which are recommended in the Appendix of this booklet, can provide us with wise, biblical, and insightful guidance as parents. In addition, we can attend conferences, listen to podcasts, read articles and blogposts, consult websites, and talk with those who have wisdom and experience in parenting. God has truly blessed us with seemingly endless resources to help us with this enormous responsibility. More than all that, God is our greatest resource. As we ask Him to show us how to care for the needs of our children, He is faithful to answer our prayers and enable us to be wise parents.

As important as it is for our children to be healthy and flourishing in every way, these promises are especially directed toward our responsibility for the spiritual development of our children. The following are five principles to guide us as we seek to fulfill this promise:

1. Keep God's Word on your heart.

One of the passages of Scripture that is foundational for our biblical responsibility as parents is Deuteronomy 6:4-9. Before commanding His people to diligently instruct their children, God says, "You shall love the LORD your God with all your heart and with all your soul and with all your might. And these words that I command you today shall be on your heart" (verse 5-6).

> **God first calls parents to wholehearted affection for Himself and His Word. From the overflow of our affection for God and His Word, we instruct our children.**

God first calls parents to wholehearted affection for Himself and His Word. From the overflow of our affection for God and His Word, we instruct our children. When God's words are on your heart, you will love them, see them to be true, live by them, and be motivated to "teach them diligently to your children and... talk of them when you sit in your house, and when you walk by the way, and when you lie down, and when you rise" (verse 7). When our own hearts are overflowing with affection for God, our children receive our teaching as more than words and our example as authentic.

Being faithful to this promise means that parents must regularly invest time and effort in their personal devotional lives. They must cultivate affection for the Lord and His Word through worship and prayerful meditation. In this promise, we commit to "looking to our own heavenly father for wisdom." The best place to find our Father's wisdom is in His Word. Generally speaking, wherever we find parents who are growing and flourishing in their faith, we will find children who are also flourishing, not only spiritually, but physically, emotionally, and intellectually as well.

2. Invest in your marriage.

> *Therefore a man shall leave his father and mother and hold fast to his wife and they shall become one flesh (Genesis 2:24).*
>
> *So God created man in his own image, in the image of God he created him; male and female he created them. And God blessed them. And God said to them, "Be fruitful and multiply and fill the earth..." (Genesis 1:27-28).*

A strong and healthy marriage is the God-ordained institution for raising physically, emotionally, intellectually, and spiritually healthy children. One of the best ways parents can provide their children with what they need is by investing in their marriage.

Among the reasons for marriage being the God-ordained institution for the rearing of children, there is one that surpasses all others, as John Piper emphasized at the end of a sermon on Ephesians 6:1-4:

> *God has ordained that both mother and father be involved in raising the children because* **they are husband and wife before they are mother and father.** *And what they are as husband and wife is where God wants children to be: As husband and wife, they are a drama of the covenant-keeping love between Christ and the church. That is where God wants children to be. His design is that children grow up watching Christ love the church and watching the church delight in following Christ. His design is that the beauty and strength and wisdom of this covenant relationship be absorbed by the children from the time they are born.*
>
> *So what turns out is that the deepest meaning of marriage—displaying the covenant love between Christ and the church—is underneath this other meaning of marriage—making children disciples of Jesus. It is all woven together. Good marriages make good places for children to grow up and see the glory of Christ's covenant-keeping love.*[17]

Both the husband and the wife play necessary roles in the rearing of children. Unique fathering from a father and unique mothering from a mother are critical in the development of a child.[18] Due to the unique roles that a husband and wife bring

---

[17] John Piper, "Marriage is Meant for Making Children Disciples of Christ, Part 1," a sermon on Ephesians 6:1-4 delivered at Bethlehem Baptist Church, Minneapolis, Minnesota, June 10, 2007. https://www.desiringgod.org/messages/marriage-is-meant-for-making-children-disciples-of-jesus-part-1

[18] Much has been written on this subject, including an insightful article by George Alan Rekers titled, "Psychological Foundations for Raising Masculine Boys and Feminine Girls," which is chapter 17 of John Piper and Wayne Grudem's book, *Recovering Biblical Manhood and Womanhood: A Response to Evangelical Feminism*. (Wheaton, Ill.: Crossway, 1991), 294-311.

to parenting, many single parents can tell us how difficult it is to raise children alone.

If this is true, where does this leave the single parent? It leaves them in the same place as every parent—dependent on "God's fatherly help." There are at least two hope-giving assurances that the Bible offers for single parents, as well as every other parent.

God compensates for our limitations; He exalts His strength in our weakness.

> But he said to me, "My grace is sufficient for you, for my power is made perfect in weakness." Therefore I will boast all the more gladly of my weaknesses, so that the power of Christ may rest upon me. For the sake of Christ, then, I am content with weaknesses . . . For when I am weak, then I am strong (2 Corinthians 12:9-10).

One of the ways God exalts His glory is to display His all-sufficiency alongside our limitations. When an army of 32,000 Israelites seemed too small to defeat the Midianite army, God's design was to reduce it to 300 and magnify His power through the weakness of man (Judges 7:2-23).

The Lord cannot be hindered or restrained from fulfilling the purpose of His will for His children.

> ". . . I am God, and there is no other; I am God and there is none like me, declaring the end from the beginning and from ancient times things not yet done, saying, 'My counsel shall stand, and I will accomplish all my purpose' . . . I have spoken, and I will bring it to pass; I have purposed, and I will do it" (Isaiah 46:9-11).

When raising children for the glory of God seems overwhelming for two parents, He is able to accomplish through a single parent "far more abundantly than all that [parents] ask or think" (Ephesians 3:20).

When the Apostle Paul was challenging the Corinthians to be generous in their giving, he told them about the Macedonians who were facing serious economic hardship ("extreme poverty") and yet they "overflowed in a "wealth of generosity" (2 Corinthians 8:2). Then Paul gave this assurance to his brothers and sisters in Corinth: "God is able to make all grace abound to you, so that having all sufficiency in all things at all times, you may abound in every good work" (2 Corinthians 9:8). This same assurance is for any single parent and any parent seeking to be faithful to this calling in the midst of hardship. God is able, and He will make all grace abound to you for His glory and the everlasting joy of your children.

3. Develop a biblical vision for discipleship.

For most parents in North America and some other parts of the world, there is no lack of opportunity for their children or resources to assist with raising them. The challenge is discerning which of the various options available to us are good for us and our children, and which are not. Even more challenging is deciding which of several good opportunities we prioritize. The way for parents to navigate the myriad of options that are available is by clarifying a vision for their children.

Psalm 127:3-5 and 1 Corinthians 3:9-17 offer two images that reinforce this vision-oriented approach to parenting. In Psalm 127:4, the psalmist describes children as "arrows in the hand of a warrior." This image suggests that the "warrior" has a target in view. Just as arrows are intended to be aimed at something, so also, in the raising of our children, we should have a specific aim or goal in view. Without a clear target, parents end up with a hit-or-miss approach to parenting, pointing their "arrows" in various directions and, at times, even in conflicting directions.

In 1 Corinthians 3:9-17, the Apostle Paul says God's people (including our children) are "God's building" (verse 9) being built on the foundation of Jesus Christ. Paul and Apollos saw themselves as builders on that foundation. Before construction on a building can begin, it is best to have a detailed vision for what that building will be. Likewise, the most effective and

> **Taking the time to develop a biblical vision unifies a husband and wife around shared goals for their children.**

fruitful parenting is governed by a biblical vision.[19]

Taking the time to develop a biblical vision unifies a husband and wife around shared goals for their children. Attempting to construct a building without a clear and specific vision of what the building should be would turn construction into chaos. So also, when parents set out to raise children without a clear sense of vision for their lives, they can be likened to a rudderless ship tossed about by every wind and whim of parental impulse.

As you begin developing a vision for discipleship, consider what you want to be true for your children when they are adults:

- What are your hopes, desires, and vision for them?
- How would you want someone to describe them when they are 20, 40, and even 60 years old?
- What do you want to be their understanding of God and the gospel?
- Who and what do you want influencing the decisions they make and the priorities of their lives?
- What habits do you envision being established?
- How would you want to be able to describe their character, their faith, and their treasure?
- What might their marriage be like?
- What would you want them to be teaching their children?

---

[19] The importance of a vision-oriented approach to the discipleship of our children is dealt with in more detail in David Michael's *Zealous: 7 Commitments for the Next Generations* (Minneapolis, Minn.: Truth78, 2020). "Embrace a biblical vision" is the first of the "7 Commitments" described in the book, starting on page 23.

- How would you hope they would handle a miscarriage, a lost job, or an argument with their spouse?
- How much Bible should they have memorized by the time they leave your home?

The first place to look for answers to these questions and others to develop a biblical vision for our children is the Bible. There are many passages that can help define our vision for our children. The first of two examples is Deuteronomy 10:12: "And now, Israel, what does the Lord your God require of you, but to fear the LORD your God, to walk in all his ways, to love him, to serve the LORD your God with all your heart and with all your soul, . . . " So 20 years from now, I am praying that my two daughters, who will be in their 50s, and my three grandchildren, who will be in their 30s, will all be fearing the Lord, walking in His ways, and loving and serving the Lord with all their hearts and souls.

A second example would be Psalm 125:1: "Those who trust in the LORD are like Mount Zion, which cannot be moved, but abides forever." Sally and I are praying that 20, 30, and 40 years from now, our children and grandchildren will be enduring in faith and remaining steadfast through the trials and suffering that come into their lives, thus proving the genuineness of their faith (1 Peter 1:7).

A helpful exercise for new parents would be to take a year to read the Bible and keep a journal noting the specific portions of God's Word that help express your vision and desires for your children. Use these verses to help express your vision for your children. This vision will influence the choices, priorities, and plans that you have for your children as they are growing up in your home.

One practical step that has helped some parents keep Promise 4 is to set aside an extended time once or twice a year to get away as a couple. This can offer a chance to experience refreshment, to pray together, to spend time in the Word together, and to take a step back to consider the state of the marriage, how each child is progressing spiritually, and any needed adjustments to goals, priorities, schedule, etc.

4. Be fully present at home.

On June 21, 1981, I experienced my first Father's Day as a dad. Among the special gifts I received was a new book by James Dobson, *Straight Talk to Men and Their Wives*. One unforgettable illustration that Dobson gave in that book influenced my fathering from that first Father's Day onward and helped shape my future ministry as a Pastor for Parenting and Family Discipleship. One point of impact was understanding the significance of my presence in the home for the sake of my children.

Dobson told the story of his firstborn turning 13 and shared an incident that, for him and Shirley, "signaled the closing of the door called 'childhood.'" Dobson then continued with this exhortation:

> *And once* [that door] *is shut, no power on earth could open it up again. That's why the toddler and elementary school years should be seen as fleeting opportunities. Yet this priceless period of influence often occurs at a time when fathers are the least accessible to their kids. They are trying to establish themselves in their occupations, racing and running and huffing and puffing, dragging home a briefcase crammed to the brim with night work, scurrying to the airport to catch the last plane to Chicago, moonlighting to pay those vacation bills, and finally collapsing in bed in a state of utter exhaustion. Another day has passed with no interchange between Dad and his teachable little boy or girl.*
>
> *One mother told me of hearing her preschool son talking to another four-year-old boy on the front steps. 'Where's your daddy?' he asked. 'I've never seen him.' 'Oh, he doesn't live here,' came the reply. 'He only sleeps here.'*
>
> *Without wanting to heap guilt on the heads of my masculine readers, I must say that too many fathers only sleep at their homes. And as a result, they have totally abdicated their*

responsibilities for leadership and influence in the lives of their children.[20]

Much has changed in our society since the summer of 1981, including the fact that it is not just dads who are "racing and running and huffing and puffing." It's both mom and dad, and consequently days, weeks, and months pass with little interaction and influence on their "teachable little boy or girl." All God's blessings—the various opportunities, activities, and resources available these days—are there to help support parents as they seek to fulfill this promise. However, none of these are meant to replace the personal and substantial involvement from both mom and dad that is required to raise our children to be physically, emotionally, intellectually, and spiritually healthy men and women of God. We dare not abdicate our God-given responsibilities for leadership and influence in the lives of our children for the sake of lesser priorities in our lives.

5. Serve and do not use him/her.

Before moving on to the last promise, we should briefly consider the final phrase of Promise 4, "looking to your own heavenly Father for the wisdom, love, and strength to serve and not use him/her."

This clause reinforces the fact that children ultimately were created by God and therefore exist for God and for His glory (Isaiah 43:6-7; Psalm 19:1), not for our personal satisfaction and pleasure. Is there satisfaction and a deep sense of personal fulfilment that parents can gain from raising their children? Certainly! Can children bring us pleasure and joy? Absolutely! Sally and I look back on our child-rearing years as the best and happiest years of our lives. Should children be expected to help with household chores and serve critical functions in the running of a household or even a family business? Of course!

As with any relationship, especially with our children, we should be more concerned about how we can serve rather than how we can be served. When we *depend* on children to fulfill an unmet need in our

---

20 James Dobson, *Straight Talk to Men and Their Wives* (Waco, Texas: Word Books, 1980), 34-35.

> **Relying on God's grace and the storehouse of His infinite blessings, we can confidently promise to provide for their physical, emotional, intellectual, and spiritual needs.**

lives, give us a sense of purpose and worth, or worse when we abuse them to satisfy our appetites and desires, we use them and offend their Creator.

18th century British Pastor John Angell James made this point when he wrote:

> ...children are something more than living domestic play-things; something more than animated household ornaments, who by their elegant accomplishments, and graceful manners, shall adorn the habitation, and be their father's pride, their mother's boast—they are the next inhabitants of our country, and the next race of friends or enemies to the cause of God on earth. The family then, I repeat, is the mold where the members of both the state and the church are cast and formed, and this ought never for a single day to be forgotten.[21]

At the end of the day, when we raise our children according to God's purpose and design for their lives—rather than imposing our selfish and idolatrous ambitions on them—our children will flourish. Relying on God's grace and the storehouse of His infinite blessings, we can confidently promise to provide for their physical, emotional, intellectual, and spiritual needs.

---

21 John Angell James, *The Church in Earnest*, Chapter 5, Section III (Boston, Mass: Gould, Kendall, & Lincoln, 1850), 116. Available online at: https://books.google.com/books?id=FuPy-dyeynW0C&printsec=frontcover&source=gbs_ge_summary_r&cad=0#v=onepage&q=play%20things&f=false

Promise 5: To pray for the salvation of our children.

Do you promise, God helping you, to make it your regular prayer that by God's grace your child will come to trust in Jesus Christ alone for the forgiveness of his/her sins and for the fulfillment of all His promises to him/her, even eternal life, and in this faith follow Jesus as Lord and obey His teachings?

There is nothing Christian parents should want more for their children than eternal life and everlasting joy in the presence of Jesus Christ. Even if, tragically, that were not our greatest desire for our children, we cannot escape our God-given responsibility as parents to faithfully raise our children in the hope of the gospel. Nor can we escape the reality that our children will only be saved by the grace of God through faith in Jesus Christ (Ephesians 2:8).

It is a sobering and humbling reality that all Christian parents are absolutely incapable of giving their children what their hearts desire most for them. We are all woefully unequal to this task. Our best efforts have no power to raise our children from spiritual death to everlasting life. We cannot turn hearts of stone into hearts of flesh. We cannot create in them the desire and the will to follow Jesus and walk in His ways. We cannot remove the sin that keeps them eternally separated from God. The most biblical vision, the best parenting strategies, and the most comprehensive Deuteronomy 6:7-9 instruction in the Christian faith does not guarantee that children will be born again and that their parents will experience the joy of seeing them walking in the truth (3 John 1:4).

Leading children to salvation is only possible with God's help and the transforming power of His grace (Luke 18:27). We can't promise that our children will become true followers of Jesus Christ. That is why this final promise must include the indispensable clause: "God helping [us], [we will] make it [our] regular prayer that by God's grace..." The most important thing I can do to provide what I desire for my children is to seek God's help and plead for His grace to accomplish what I am powerless to do in the heart of my child. This is a promise to pray.

Pray Earnestly

To be seriously committed to keeping the first four dedication promises means being seriously committed to the fifth—namely to pray earnestly, regularly, and biblically for the faith of the next generation. God's power in the gospel of Jesus Christ, His unstoppable purposes for our children, and our inescapable responsibility to raise them in the faith all come together in prayer.

The night before Jesus was crucified, He told Peter, "Satan demanded to have you, that he might sift you like wheat, but I have prayed for you that your faith may not fail" (Luke 22:31-32). Isn't that amazing? Jesus, the Son of God, who sustains the universe by the word of His power, felt compelled to pray that Peter's faith would not fail. This was after He had declared with absolute authority that this same man was the rock on which "I will build my church, and the gates of hell shall not prevail against it" (Matthew 16:18).

The commitment to pray for the next generations, or for anything else, is best served by establishing a regular pattern or habit of prayer—private prayer, parental prayer, and family prayer. Home life provides many opportunities and ways to pray for children. In our home, I had the privilege of praying over our girls almost every night before they went to sleep.

As I was praying on one of those nights in the spring of 1991, an overwhelming sense of inadequacy came over me as I considered what I desired most for Amy and Kristi, alongside my profound limitations as a dad. I concluded that prayer with the benediction from Numbers 6:24-26,

> **The commitment to pray for the next generations, or for anything else, is best served by establishing a regular pattern or habit of prayer—private prayer, parental prayer, and family prayer.**

> *The LORD bless you and keep you;*
> *the LORD make his face to shine on you*
> *and be gracious to you;*
> *the LORD lift up his countenance upon you*
> *and give you peace.*

From that evening forward, almost without exception, my final fatherly privilege of the day was to place my right hand on each daughter's head and pronounce a biblical benediction (blessing) over them. In each of those moments, my daughters witnessed their daddy express his dependence on God for the fulfillment of his heart's desire and vision for their lives.

Sally's prayer life has been heavily weighted toward praying for the faith of our children and grandchildren. Several decades ago, she wrote *Praying for the Next Generation,* a guide to praying Scripture, which is her favorite way to pray for the next generation. We should never minimize the eternal impact of a mother's faithful prayers for the faith of her children.

Pray Regularly

For decades, I have been inspired by the example of George McClusky, who lived more than 150 years ago. He, like me, was the father of two daughters. He also was a man who understood that he could not provide what he desired most for his daughters. At some point after his daughters, Bessie and Allie, were born, George resolved to devote himself to praying daily from 11 a.m. to noon, not only for the spiritual welfare of his daughters but also for their children and their children's children. Only God knows all the fruit that came from those prayers, but there is substantial evidence that God's ear was inclined to hear the faithful prayers of George McClusky.

Bessie and Allie grew up, came to trust Jesus, and followed Him as Lord. The men they married both became pastors, and soon George was praying for his four granddaughters and one grandson. The four granddaughters all married pastors, and the grandson became a pastor. The first two of George's great grandchildren were both boys. One was H.B. London, who spent 30 years as a local pastor serving congregations in Oregon and California, and then 20 more years serving clergy families through his "Pastor to Pastor" ministry, before retiring and serving for another seven years as a local pastor until his death in 2018.

London's older cousin, George's first great-grandchild, did not become a pastor. Instead, he pursued a career in psychology, began writing books for Christian parents, founded a family ministry, and hosted a daily radio program that was eventually broadcast in more than a dozen languages on more than 7,000 stations worldwide. The program was heard daily by more than 220 million people in 164 countries, and he became the man who during the '80s and '90s was undoubtedly the most influential and significant leader of the pro-family movement that swept across America.

The Kingdom influence of that man, James Dobson, and his cousin, H.B. London, not to mention the influence of their forefathers and their descendants, is owing to God's inclination to hear the prayers of a faithful dad from five generations earlier.[22]

Pray Biblically

I would be surprised if any Christian parent reading this would disagree with the importance of praying for our children. Many parents will say, "I pray for my children all the time," and I have no doubt that it is true. After years of listening to the prayers of parents and grandparents for their children, realizing how anemic my own prayers were for my children and grandchildren, and reading a book on prayer that challenged me and convicted me to pray more intentionally, I wrote a little book titled, *Big, Bold, Biblical Prayers for the Next Generation*. That book includes all that I would want to say here, not only about why prayer is indispensable to our parenting efforts but also practical help for praying intentionally for our children. It includes examples of prayers that can help parents learn how to pray more biblically and boldly for their children. I commend this resource to you.

---

22 To read Dobson's full account of his great grandfather's influence on his family see: James Dobson, *Your Legacy: The Greatest Gift* (New York, Boston, Nashville: Faith Words, 2014).

Pray Dependently

Ephesians 2:8-9 affirms that saving faith for any child "is the gift of God, not a result of works, so that no [parent, grandparent, pastor, or Sunday school teacher] may boast." God's unstoppable purposes for our children and our inescapable responsibility to raise them in the faith come together in prayer. May God help us make it "our regular prayer that by God's grace our child will come to trust in Jesus Christ alone for the forgiveness of his/her sins and for the fulfillment of all His promises to them, even eternal life; and in this faith follow Jesus as Lord and obey His teachings."

A Time for Commitment and Dedication

Whether or not you have or are planning to dedicate your child(ren) in your church, making public your gratitude to God for the child(ren) He has given you and your pledge to parental faithfulness is a good thing. Even though, as stated above, there is no biblical mandate to dedicate your children in this way, I think it is a wise and helpful step for parents to take. If your church does not offer a dedication service, I would suggest coming together with your spouse and a small group of friends or family members to make these promises aloud and pray for God's grace to keep them.

In the dedication services that I have led, usually the parents are standing in front of the congregation with the child(ren) they are dedicating. After some brief words of preparation for the parents and the congregation, the presiding pastor directs his attention to the parents, asking them to respond with the words, "I do"[23] to the following five questions:

1. Do you recognize these children as a gift of God and give heartfelt thanks for God's blessing?

2. Do you dedicate these children to the Lord who gave them to you, surrendering all worldly claims upon their lives in the hope that they will belong wholly to Jesus Christ?

3. Do you pledge, with God's fatherly help, to bring up these children in the discipline and instruction of the Lord, making every effort, with faithfulness, patience, and love, to build the Word of God, the character of Christ, and the joy of the Lord into their lives?

---

[23] Even though it may seem more natural for a parent couple to say, "We do," it is important to understand that we make these promises as individuals. If our spouse dies, leaves the marriage, or shirks his or her responsibility, we are still called to be a faithful parent.

4. Do you promise to provide, through God's blessing, for the physical, emotional, intellectual, and spiritual needs of your children, looking to your own heavenly Father for the wisdom, love, and strength to serve and not use them?

5. Do you promise, God helping you, to make it your regular prayer that, by God's grace, your children will come to trust in Jesus Christ alone for the forgiveness of their sins and for the fulfillment of all His promises to them, even eternal life; and in this faith follow Jesus as Lord and obey His teachings?

After commitments are made to the promises, there are two other parts of the service, both of which are privileges and highlights for me. The first is when I place my right hand on the back of each child's head, look into his/her eyes and say,

Together with your parents who love you dearly and this congregation that cares about the outcome of your faith, I dedicate you to God, surrendering together with them all worldly claim upon your life in the hope that you will belong wholly to Jesus Christ forever.

"Together" is a powerful word in this context. After making these significant promises and committing ourselves to more than what we can do on our own, this word reminds us that we are not alone. The vision and hope for this child belonging "wholly to Jesus Christ forever" is a shared desire. As parents, we have two partners standing with us and supporting us as we seek to raise our children.

One of the partners in this vision and hope is "this congregation"—the people standing with the parents and sharing in hope for their children. After pronouncing these words of dedication, I usually say, "And all the people said . . . Amen!" Beforehand, the congregation is reminded that their "Amen" means that they intend to support, encourage, pray for, and help these parents keep the promises we have made for the sake of our children.

God has provided parents with a community to support and pray for them as they carry out their responsibility to instruct their children in the truth of God's Word. This same community is a place where our children can find other godly examples to imitate.

Nursery workers and Sunday school teachers in the church can also have significant influence on our children and, alongside the parents, have a shared vision for the discipleship of the children in their care. The nursery ministry has potential to be far more than childcare for the church. It can be one of the most fruitful discipleship ministries of the church by providing a foundation of prayer and simple truths for your children.[24]

The other and foremost partner in this vision and hope is God, who is committed to declaring His glory from one generation to the next and to fulfilling His unstoppable purposes to raise up worshipers in every generation. If God is for us and for our children, we have all we need!

The other highlight for me is the final prayer of dedication, which over the years has given me the opportunity to express my pastor's heart for the children, the parents, and the congregation. At the close of the prayer, it has been my custom to lift my hands above the children, attempt to look each of them in the eye again, and pronounce a biblical benediction over them. Many of the sample prayers in the book, *Big, Bold, Biblical, Prayers for the Next Generation* were originally prepared as prayers of dedication. Most of the benedictions were first prepared for my own children and can be found in *A Father's Guide to Blessing His Children*. (See the resource list in the Appendix for more information.)

As I conclude this little book, I would like to share the following prayer of dedication and benediction that I prayed at the dedication of our second grandchild, Katherine Joy Steward. Not only is this a fresh reminder to me of my hope and desire for Katie, her big sister, and her little brother, but it is also my heart and prayer for you, dear reader, and your children, in the hope that they will belong wholly to Jesus Christ, forever.

---

[24] A resource that may be helpful in transforming your nursery ministry from a childcare service to a spiritual ministry is *A Sure Foundation*. See the resource list in the Appendix of the booklet for more information on this resource.

Almighty God,

Please grant to Amy and Gary [Katie's parents] and to this congregation the grace they need to keep the promises they just made. What they will need, only You know.

The outcome of Katie's life, the course that it will take is unknown to us but there are many things we do know and are certain of this morning.

We are certain that she was created for Your glory.

We are certain that Your eyes are on the righteous and Your ears are attentive to their cries.

We are certain that those who hear the Word of God and obey it are blessed.

We are certain that if she calls on the name of the Lord, she will be saved.

We are certain that You cause all things to work together for good to those who love You, to those who are called according to Your purpose.

So Lord,

> *more than wealth or fame,*
>
> *more than a good education and a good job,*
>
> *and a nice home and a strong family,*
>
> *more than health,*
>
> *more than friends and a good husband someday,*
>
> *more than a long and fruitful life,*

we pray that Katie will be born again and called according to Your purpose.

We pray that You will open her eyes to see her need and give her the will and the power to call upon the name of the Lord her God.

Lord, we have this morning, surrendered all worldly claim on her life.

Take everything from her if You must, but give her Jesus...

And now Katie, may you become a woman who fears the Lord,

A woman who finds great delight in the Lord's commands.

May your children be mighty in the land.

Even to the next generation may you and your children be blessed.

May you find your wealth and your riches in God.

May you endure in righteousness forever.

Even in the darkness may the light dawn for you.

May you abound in

> *love, joy, peace,*
>
> *patience, kindness, goodness,*
>
> *faithfulness, gentleness, and self-control.*

May you never be shaken.

And may your name, Katherine Joy Steward, be remembered by the Lord forever!

And all the people said, "Amen!"

Appendix 1

Exposition of Ephesians 6:4[25]

John Piper

Fathers, do not provoke your children to anger, but bring them up in the discipline and instruction of the Lord.

Even though *both* mother and father work together in raising the children ("children obey your *parents*," v. 1), fathers are the special focus of verse 4. Fathers have a leading responsibility for raising children. This is a natural extension of the headship of the wife in Ephesians 5:23-25. Dad should take the initiative to make sure that plans and processes and people are in place to build a vision of God and truth and holiness into the lives of the children.

...bring them up... (*ektrephete auta*)

This word means most basically *to provide for*—especially with nourishment. But it comes to have a broader sense of rearing children with a connotation of care. The solicitous feel to the word shows up in Ephesians 5:29 where Paul says, "No one ever hated his own flesh, but *nourishes* and cherishes it." That word *nourishes* is the same word as *bring up* in Ephesians 6:4. So the focus is on the fact that, in all that a father does to bring his children to maturity there should be a provision and a care that assures the child that, behind all the discipline and instruction, there is a great heart of love. This earthly father is working all things together for the good of his child. And so God's character is being displayed.

---

25 John Piper, "More Thoughts for Fathers on Ephesians 6:4:The Part of the Sermon that Didn't Get Preached," June 20, 1997, https://www.desiringgod.org/articles/more-thoughts-for-fathers-on-ephesians-6-4

...in the discipline... (*paideia*)

This word signifies the actions a father takes to give his children the abilities and skills and character to live life to the glory of God. It is not synonymous with teaching. It is more full and more active. For example, it is used in 2 Timothy 3:16 for "training." "All Scripture is breathed out by God and profitable for teaching, for reproof, for correction, and for *training* in righteousness." Notice that "teaching" is mentioned earlier in the verse. "Training" involves the action of the one being trained and then the helpful consequences of doing poorly or well.

So the word often refers to the painful part of training: "It is for *discipline* that you have to endure. God is treating you as sons. For what son is there whom his father does not discipline? If you are left without *discipline*, in which all have participated, then you are illegitimate children and not sons" (Hebrews 12:7-8). Growing up with a Christian father's help involves being shown how to do the things that a Christ-exalting life requires and being held accountable to do them as well as you can.

...and instruction... (*nouthesia*)

This word is not the ordinary word for "teaching" (*didaskalian*). "Instruction" does not quite capture the force of this word. In fact, it is used alongside of the word *teaching* as different from it in Colossians 1:28: "[Christ] we proclaim, *warning* everyone and teaching everyone with all wisdom, that we may present everyone mature in Christ." The idea of *warning* is prominent. One major Greek lexicon defines the word like this: "to counsel about avoidance or cessation of an improper course of conduct."

We can see the corrective, warning side of this word in 1 Thessalonians 5:14 where Paul says, "We urge you, brothers, *admonish* the idle, encourage the fainthearted, help the weak, be patient with them all." What the idle need is something a little different than the fainthearted. That is called *admonish*—a corrective warning about the fruitlessness of this kind of laziness.

But Paul is keen to make sure we feel the sweetness in the admonition he has in mind. Catch the feel of the word in these two verses:

1 Corinthians 4:14, "I do not write these things to make you ashamed, but to *admonish* you as my beloved children"; 2 Thessalonians 3:15, "Do not regard him as an enemy, but *warn* him as a brother." There is a warmth to the correcting, warning, and guiding that fathers are called to do. You can even sing it. And fathers should sing it: "Let the word of Christ dwell in you richly, teaching and *admonishing* one another in all wisdom, singing psalms and hymns and spiritual songs, with thankfulness in your hearts to God" (Colossians 3:16).

...of the Lord. *(kuriou)*

This modifies the training and the admonition. "Bring them up in the discipline and admonition *of the Lord*." I take it to mean that the *content* of a father's teachings and warnings, and the *method* of a father's modeling discipline, and the *goal* of a father's whole life with his children will be from the Lord, through the Lord, and for the Lord. That is, a father will guide all his words and ways by God's *word*, and depend on God's *wisdom* and *strength* to apply them, and make everything serve the *glory* of Christ. In other words, the most important thing in raising children is that they come to see Christ, the Lord, as supremely valuable as Savior and Lord and Treasure of life. Everything is measured by how that might be biblically achieved.

O Lord, grant to all of us fathers to lead our children (even our adult children) ever more faithfully to love Christ above all.

Appendix 2

Recommended Resources

Bettis, Chap. *The Disciple-Making Parent: A Comprehensive Guidebook for Raising Your Children to Love and Follow Jesus.* (Cumberland, R.I.: Diamond Hill Publishing, 2016).

> From the back cover: *Your children will either live forever with Jesus or apart from him...In the* Disciple-Making Parent, *you will discover:*
>
> a. *The North Star to Guide Your Parenting*
> b. *The Process Second-Generation Christians Go Through*
> c. *The Reasons Young People Walk Away from the Faith*
> d. *Nine Powerful Influences Found in Wise Families*
> e. *The Doubts Your Children Will Experience and What You Can Do*

Crotts, John. *Mighty Men: The Starter's Guide to Leading Your Family.* (Sand Springs, Okla.: Grace and Truth Books, 2000).

> From the back cover: *Christian men often find the task of family leadership so daunting that we withdraw from it into a distant uninvolvement, leaving our wives and children with the impression that we don't care enough to lead, or don't want to—when the heart of the problem is, we're simply frightened by the task of our God-given responsibility.*
>
> *John Crotts' book is written with the hope of providing a "starter kit" for men who have been reluctant to take the reins of spiritual leadership in their homes, and show them the path to imitating Christ in loving, servant leadership.*

Farley, William P. *Gospel-Powered Parenting: How the Gospel Shapes and Transforms Parenting*. (Phillipsburg, N.J.: P&R Publishing Company, 2009).

> From the back cover: *Parents who claim the gospel as their own have an enormous effect on their marriage, their integrity, and their love for their children. Keeping the gospel at the forefront of every aspect of marriage helps parents fear God, sensitizes them to sin, motivates them to enter their children's world, and causes them to preach the beauty of the gospel to their children through their marriage.*

Gundersen, Dennis. *Your Child's Profession of Faith*. (Amityville, N.Y.: Calvary Press, 1994).

> From the back cover: *This unique, helpful work addresses one of a Christian parent's greatest dilemmas: should I take my child's profession of faith at face value? Is this real conversion, or is it possible that my child is deceived?...*
>
> *Here's a book which directly explores these difficult questions, ones rarely addressed in a truly practical manner in either Christian literature or preaching. Whether we are parents, pastors, or educators, having biblical balanced answers to these issues is essential to our work among children. Your use of this unique guide to a child's profession of faith can make all the difference between having a child who is lastingly sealed in self-deception or one with a well-reasoned, growing assurance.*

Michael, David. *A Father's Guide to Blessing His Children*. (Minneapolis, Minn.: Truth78, 2009).

> From the back cover: *God faithfully hears and remembers your blessings. Speaking a blessing over your children in the presence of God allows you to intentionally seek God's favor, grace, and power to flow through you into their lives.*
>
> *As your children hear you bless them day after day you will have the opportunity to express what you desire most for them—that they fear the LORD and delight to do His will. They can hear the hope that the LORD will be their counselor all the days of their*

lives and can catch a vision for having their names remembered by the LORD forever.

A Father's Guide to Blessing His Children *equips and encourages fathers to establish a routine of blessing their children. This booklet includes 29 blessings that are rooted in Scripture and flow from the heart of a father and pastor who wants to bless his children and the next generations in his church.*

Michael, David. *Big, Bold, Biblical Prayers for the Next Generation.* (Minneapolis, Minn.: Truth78, 2019).

From the website and back cover: *Prayer matters! It matters to us. It matters to our children. It matters to every generation until Jesus comes. It matters because God is pleased to accomplish His unstoppable purposes through the prayers of His people. The needs of the next generation, the challenges they face, and the opportunities before them are great. What might God be pleased to do if His people come to Him with BIG, BOLD, BIBLICAL prayers of faith?*

This booklet imparts a vision for praying for the next generations; explains what a big, bold, biblical prayer is; provides sample big, bold biblical prayers; and lists verses to use in praying for the next generations.

Michael, David. *Established in the Faith: A Discipleship Guide for Discerning and Affirming A Young Person's Faith.* (Minneapolis, Minn.: Truth78, 2018).

From the back cover: *In our disciple-making efforts, it can be difficult to discern if someone is born again and thus a true disciple of Jesus Christ. This is especially true for children growing up in Christian homes and in the church. Children can know all the right words to say, give all the correct answers to our questions, sincerely confess faith in Christ, and still be dead in their sins (Ephesians 2:1) with hearts far from God (Isaiah 29:13).*

This guide is recommended for use with young people age 11 and older who profess faith in Christ. The six-step process outlined will assist parents and others to help their young disciples examine themselves to see whether they "are in the faith" (2 Corinthians 13:5).

Michael, David. *Zealous: 7 Commitments for the Discipleship of the Next Generations.* (Minneapolis, Minn.: Truth78, 2020).

> From the back cover: *"Do not be slothful in zeal," the apostle Paul urges, "be fervent in spirit, serve the Lord." The next generation needs parents, teachers, and church leaders who are zealous for their discipleship. But where does zeal come from? And what does zealous discipleship look like day to day?*
>
> *In* Zealous, *long-time pastor and Truth78 Executive Director David Michael describes a fervor and diligence born out of a passion for God and His glory and presents seven commitments that provide a vision and framework for the discipleship of the next generations...so that they should set their hope in God (Psalm 78:1-8).*

Michael, Sally. *A Sure Foundation: A Philosophy and Curriculum for Ministry to Infants and Toddlers.* (Minneapolis, Minn.: Truth78, 2005, 2017).

> *Nursery and toddler ministry is more than providing childcare. It is a spiritual ministry. However, it is not often seen as part of the church's discipleship training.* A Sure Foundation *will help you to transform your nurseries into a place for prayer, where children learn simple truths about God, begin to memorize Scripture, and hear foundational Bible stories.*

Michael, Sally, Jill Nelson, and Bud Burk. *Helping Children to Understand the Gospel.* (Minneapolis, Minn.: Truth78, 2009, 2019).

> From the back cover: *"A sower went out to sow..." Thus begins one of the most familiar parables from Jesus' teaching. But how should parents and teachers apply the teaching of Matthew 13 as they parent and teach their children? The gospel is the most important truth one generation can communicate to the next, and God calls parents and teachers to be wise sowers. This calls for accurate, discerning, and intentional practices of cultivating, teaching, and praying in the hope that God, who gives the growth, will work in children's hearts to yield hundredfold harvests of*

faith. This booklet includes a 10-week family devotional and 10 Essential Gospel Truths to help parents explain the gospel to their children. Other topics explored include: preparing the hearts of children to hear the gospel, discerning stages of spiritual growth, communicating the essential truths of the gospel, and presenting the gospel in an accurate and child-friendly manner.

Michael, Sally. *Mothers: Disciplers of the Next Generations.* (Minneapolis, Minn.: Truth78, 2013).

From the back cover: *Mothering is a great work—a God-given opportunity to influence the next generations to put their trust in God. Do we see it as such? Do we awake each day with the anticipation of the opportunity God has given us to impart the words of life, to nurture budding seeds of faith, to lead our little ones to the Savior?*

Sally Michael's prayer in writing this booklet is that it will challenge you to look on your mothering with a biblical perspective to seize the opportunities God gives you each day to encourage faith in your children, and to rely on Him as your Sin-bearer and Enabler to do the great work He has called you to do.

Michael, Sally. *Praying for the Next Generation.* (Minneapolis, Minn.: Truth78, 2006).

From the back cover: *What kind of legacy do you want to leave for the children in your life? Sally Michael encourages you to consider the spiritual inheritance you can give to the next generation through your faithful prayers, and equips you with a method for using Scripture to pray for your child, grandchild, or the children in your church.*

Murphy, Art. *The Faith of a Child: A Step-by-Step Guide to Salvation for Your Child.* (Chicago, Ill.: Moody Press, 2000).

From the back cover: *Most parents, teachers, and pastors wrestle with the prickly issue of children and salvation. The good news is that we don't have to. God wants us to be equipped and confident in doing <u>our</u> part to lead our children to a genuine relationship with Jesus Christ.*

> *Written by a children's pastor, this book includes practical instruction on:*
> - *the stages of your child's spiritual development*
> - *the signs that your child is ready to become a Christian*
> - *taking your child's spiritual temperature*
> - *witnessing to a child*

Plowman, Ginger. *Don't Make Me Count to Three: A Mom's Look at Heart-Oriented Discipline*. (Wapwallopen, Pa.: Shepherd Press, 2004).

> From the back cover: *Through personal experience and the practical application of Scripture, Ginger Plowman encourages and equips moms to reach past the outward behavior of their children and dive deeply into the issues of the heart.*

Priolo, Lou. *Teach Them Diligently*. (Woodruff, S.C.: Timeless Texts, 2000).

> From the back cover: *With rare exception...most of today's Christian parenting resources fail to emphasize what is perhaps the most important aspect of true biblical parenting—how to relate the Bible to the disciplinary process in practical ways.*

Ryle, J.C. *The Duties of Parents*. (Sand Springs, Okla.: Grace & Truth Books, originally published in 1888).

> From the back cover: *I know...that God says expressly, 'Train up a child in the way he should go,' and that He never laid a command on man which He would not give man the grace to perform. And I know too, that our duty is not to stand still and dispute, but to go forward and obey. It is just in the going forward that God will meet us. The path to obedience is the way in which He gives the blessing.*
>
> *Bishop Ryle does an excellent job of expounding the principles of God's Word which greatly need to be practiced in this day.*

Tripp, Ted and Margy. *Instructing a Child's Heart.* (Wapwallopen, Pa.: Shepherd Press, 2008).

> From the back cover: Instructing a Child's Heart *is essential to Shepherding a Child's Heart. The instruction that you provide for them not only informs their mind; it is directed to persuading their hearts of the wisdom and truthfulness of God's ways. Impress truth on the hearts of your children, not to control or manage them, but to point them to the greatest joy and happiness that they can experience—delighting in God and the goodness of his ways.*

Tripp, Ted. *Shepherding A Child's Heart.* (Wapwallopen, Pa.: Shepherd Press, 1995).

> From the back cover: Shepherding a Child's Heart *is about how to speak to the heart of your child. The things your child does and says flow from their heart. Luke 6:45 puts it this way, "out of the overflow of the heart the mouth speaks." (NIV) Written for parents with children of any age, this insightful book provides perspectives and procedures for shepherding your child's heart into the paths of life.*

Trumbull, H. Clay. *Hints on Child Training.* (Eugene, Ore.: Great Expectations Book Co, 1993). (This book was originally published in 1890.)

> *This book, written more than 100 years ago, is still relevant today. As a minister with decades of dealing with children, Trumbull shares common-sense wisdom and a wealth of practical insights into the training of children.*

Appendix 3

Truth:78

TRUTH78 is a vision-oriented ministry for the next generations—that they may know, honor, and treasure God, setting their hope in Christ alone, so that they will live as faithful disciples for the glory of God.

Our mission is to nurture the faith of the next generations by equipping the church and home with resources and training that instruct the mind, engage the heart, and influence the will through proclaiming the whole counsel of God.

Equip Your Church and Home

Truth78 offers the following categories of resources and training materials for the church and home:

Vision-Casting and Training

We offer opportunities to grow in biblical vision, encouragement, and practical applications for ministry to the next generations through a wide variety of booklets, video and audio seminars, articles, and other practical training resources that highlight and expound our vision, mission, and values, as well as our educational philosophy and methodology. Many of these resources are freely distributed through our website to help ministry leaders, volunteers, and parents implement Truth78's vision and mission in their churches and homes. By subscribing to the Truth78 e-newsletter (Truth78.org/enewsletter), you will receive weekly updates on new articles and resources.

Curriculum

We publish materials designed for formal Bible instruction. The scope and sequence of these materials reflects our commitment to teach children and youth the whole counsel of God over the course of their education. Materials include curricula for Sunday schools, midweek Bible programs, Backyard Bible Clubs or vacation Bible schools, and intergenerational studies. Most of these materials can be adapted for use in Christian schools and education in the home. Learn more at Truth78.org/curriculum-introduction.

Parenting and Family Discipleship

We have produced a variety of materials and training resources designed to help parents disciple their children, including booklets, video presentations, family devotionals, children's books, and articles. Our curricula also include parent pages to help apply what is taught in the classroom to their children's daily experience in order to nurture faith. Learn more at Truth78.org/family-overview.

Bible Memory

Our Fighter Verses™ Bible memory program is designed to encourage churches, families, and individuals in the lifelong practice and love of Bible memory. The program offers an easy-to-use Bible memory system with carefully chosen verses to help fight the fight of faith. It is available in print, on FighterVerses.com, and as an app for smartphones and other mobile devices (IOS and Android in English, Spanish, French, and German). The Fighter Verses app includes review systems, quizzes, songs, a devotional, and other memory helps. For pre-readers, Foundation Verses uses simple images to help young children memorize 76 key verses. We also offer a study that corresponds to Set One of the Fighter Verses. Visit FighterVerses.com for more on the Fighter Verses Study, as well as a weekly devotional blog and free memory aids. See Truth78.org/products for more details on all Truth78 resources.

Partner with Truth78

There is a global need for solid biblical teaching that points the next generation to the glorious character and works of God so that they might "set their hope in God" and walk in His ways. Our commitment is to provide biblically sound resources for children and youth, as well as training materials that will not only serve North America but those around the world. Will you help spread the testimony and the "glorious deeds" of God to the next generation so they may "set their hope in God"?

Pray

Would you join us in making bold requests to the Lord?

- Pray that one generation will declare God's Word to the next and give us, as part of this generation, the grace to faithfully fulfill our responsibility and calling to the next.
- Pray that the Lord of the Harvest would send out workers into His harvest and equip us with all we need to do His will, keeping our hands to the plow until His work through us is done.
- Pray that the next generation will know and honor Jesus as their eternal treasure.
- Pray for increasing numbers of individuals, churches, and schools who are able to benefit from our resources.
- Pray for the continued efforts of translation teams and the establishment of new translation partners so that children around the world will have resources in their native language.
- Pray that the Lord would multiply praying and giving partners so that a rich harvest would be experienced by millions around the world.
- Pray for a growing network of individuals, churches, and Christian educators who are zealous for the discipleship of the next generation.

Give

Approximately 70% of our budget is funded through the sale of our resources. The other 30% is provided as God leads people to partner with us financially. This strategy allows us to fulfill our commitment to serve the Church while giving our partners who share this mission an opportunity to increase the impact of our ministry. Financial gifts allow for greater capacity to spread the vision broadly, produce affordable discipleship resources for the church and home, provide training to equip ministry leaders and parents, and distribute materials for our under-resourced brothers and sisters in North America and internationally. We invite you to partner with us in this effort. Truth78 is a 501(c)(3) nonprofit ministry, making your gift tax deductible. You can find out more about giving at Truth78.org/donate. For more information on resources and training materials contact:

Truth78.org
info@Truth78.org
877.400.1414
@Truth78org